How To Hook Rugs

Christine Brault

4880 Lower Valley Road   Atglen, Pennsylvania 19310

Other Schiffer Books on Related Subjects
The Big Book of Hooked Rugs: 1950-1980s. Jessie A. Turbayne.
Contemporary Hooked Rugs: Themes and Memories. Linda Rae Coughlin.
The Creative Hooker. Jessie A. Turbayne.
Hooked on Rugs: Outstanding Contemporary Designs. Jessie Turbayne.
Hooked Rugs Today: Holidays, Geometrics, People, Animals, Landscapes, Accessories, and More -- 2006. Amy Oxford.
Hooked Rugs Today: Strong Women, Flowers, Animals, Children, Christmas, Miniatures, and More -- 2006. Amy Oxford.
The Hooker's Art: Evolving Designs in Hooked Rugs. Jessie A. Turbayne.
Modern Hooked Rugs. Linda Rae Coughlin.

Copyright © 2008 by Christine J. Brault
Library of Congress Control Number: 2001012345

All rights reserved. No part of this work may be reproduced or used in any form or by any means—graphic, electronic, or mechanical, including photocopying or information storage and retrieval systems—without written permission from the publisher.

The scanning, uploading and distribution of this book or any part thereof via the Internet or via any other means without the permission of the publisher is illegal and punishable by law. Please purchase only authorized editions and do not participate in or encourage the electronic piracy of copyrighted materials.

"Schiffer," "Schiffer Publishing Ltd. & Design," and the "Design of pen and ink well" are registered trademarks of Schiffer Publishing Ltd.

Type set in University Roman Bd BT/News Gothic BT

ISBN: 978-0-7643-2890-9
Printed in China

Schiffer Books are available at special discounts for bulk purchases for sales promotions or premiums. Special editions, including personalized covers, corporate imprints, and excerpts can be created in large quantities for special needs. For more information contact the publisher:

Published by Schiffer Publishing Ltd.
4880 Lower Valley Road
Atglen, PA 19310
Phone: (610) 593-1777; Fax: (610) 593-2002
E-mail: Info@schifferbooks.com

For the largest selection of fine reference books on this and related subjects, please visit our web site at **www.schifferbooks.com**
We are always looking for people to write books on new and related subjects. If you have an idea for a book please contact us at the above address.

This book may be purchased from the publisher.
Include $3.95 for shipping.
Please try your bookstore first.
You may write for a free catalog.

In Europe, Schiffer books are distributed by
Bushwood Books
6 Marksbury Ave.
Kew Gardens
Surrey TW9 4JF England
Phone: 44 (0) 20 8392-8585; Fax: 44 (0) 20 8392-9876
E-mail: info@bushwoodbooks.co.uk
Website: www.bushwoodbooks.co.uk
Free postage in the U.K., Europe; air mail at cost.

Contents

Schiffer Publishing
Your Source for
Books on Crafts

Shorebird Carving–Rosalyn Daisey
8 1/2" x 11", 207 color, 611 b/w photos, 256 pp.
ISBN: 0-88740-219-4, hard cover, $49.95

Favorite Santas for Carvers–Ron Ransom
Size: 8 1/2" x 11", 225 color photos, 64 pp.
ISBN: 0-7643-2362-8, soft cover, $12.95

Carving Caricature Heads–W. "Pete" LeClair
8 1/2" x 11", 33 caricature carvings, 64 pp.
ISBN: 0-88740-784-6, soft cover, $12.95

Dick Sing Turns Miniature Birdhouses
8 1/2" x 11", 395 color photos, 80 pp.
ISBN: 0-7643-2080-7, soft cover, $14.95

Pens From the Wood Lathe–Dick Sing
8 1/2" x 11", 273 photos, 64 pp.
ISBN: 0-88740-939-3, soft cover, $12.95

Constructing a Fireplace Mantel–Steve
Penberthy
8 1/2" x 11", 330 color photos, 64 pp.
ISBN: 0-7643-2457-8, soft cover, $14.95

Making Mobiles–Bruce Cana Fox
8 1/2" x 11", 199 color photos, 80 pp.
ISBN: 0-7643-2474-8, soft cover, $14.95

For our complete catalog of books visit
www.schifferbooks.com
C-2

Acknowledgments

First, I want to thank my wonderful family: my husband, Mike, who let's me run with my off-the-wall creations and my constantly changing ideas; my kids, Peter, Elaine, and stepson, Matt, for their patience with the disheveled household. Special thanks to Mike for taking over the grocery shopping and cooking so that I could write and hook.

I am extremely grateful to my parents, Robert and Tina Clifford, for always supporting and encouraging me in all my endeavors. My mother has always been my biggest cheerleader and my father has always provided practical, sound advice.

Great thanks to Rich Maclone of capecodportrait.com for the photos and his wonderful wife, Nancy, for her work on the final photos.

Thank you to Nancy Condon, who first showed me the art of rug hooking; Norma McElhenny and Diane Stoeffel, for their great classes and color advice. Thanks to Mike of Spohr Gardens in Falmouth, Massachusetts, for letting us use the beautiful gardens for some of the vignette photos. There is more information about Spohr's Garden at the back of the book.

And thanks to the people who constantly encourage me – Denis Brault, Denise Almeida, Liz Miller, Dinah Clark, Judy Gaseidnes, and Betty Corbett. Special thanks to Denise for her proofreading and grammar correction!

Foreword

With Hook In Hand

From the first time that I discovered glue and glitter in kindergarten, I have always loved making things with my hands. There is nothing so satisfying as the feeling you get when you finish a project and proudly think, "WOW! This was fun!"

I learned to sew when I was in elementary school and began sewing my own figure skating outfits and ballet skirts. I started painting and doing all kinds of crafts as a kid and knew that I wanted to work in an artistic field. I earned my degree in culinary arts but continued with quilting and painting. When I became a stay at home mom I taught decorative painting and faux finishes at a local community school.

One day, many years ago, a painting student of mine showed me a project she was working on. It was a Claire Murray rug of a Cape Cod cottage. My heart started beating faster and fireworks exploded in my head! This was incredible! Oh my goodness – the softness of the yarn, the gorgeous design, the simple technique! How had I not discovered this before?! It was so beautiful and so easy. I immediately went to a Claire Murray store and bought a kit. I was in heaven! That first rug is still a favorite sleeping spot for my dogs.

My first rug was hooked with yarn in a style known as "Nantucket." Very fitting since I'm from Cape Cod! Nantucket style is tucking the backing fabric around your thighs so that your lap is the frame. I loved this because I could take it everywhere and it gave me a cozy feeling in the winter. Later I began using a sit-on gripper frame, but sometimes when I want to feel warm and fuzzy I go back to the Nantucket style.

Introduction

Rug Hooking

How creative our ancestors must have been to see a burlap bag and strips of wool as a beautiful rug! Necessity may have been the mother of invention but today the art of rug hooking has gone from functional (keeping our tootsies warm) to a fascinating fiber art of pillows, dolls, bags – the list is endless.

Hooking is actually a very simple concept – stick the hook through the hole, catch a piece of wool fabric or length of wool yarn, and pull up a loop, repeat, repeat, repeat. Rug hooking is a great hobby because you can make it as challenging as you want. If you find primitives relaxing, you can continue with primitives, but if you want a challenge, you can go on to more advanced projects.

While I love primitives, I have tried to include projects here which will fit with other decors. My daughter, Elaine, inspired the peace rug and "funky" pillows. We live near the ocean, which inspired "Stay The Course" and the beach tote. A colorful dinner plate gave me the idea for "With a Song in My Heart." Ideas can come from anywhere!

Supplies

Rug hooking only takes a few basic supplies – backing fabric, hooking tool, and hooking material. There are projects in this book to get you started. After that, you are only limited by your own imagination. ANYTHING can become a hooked design.

Backing Fabrics

Let's start with the backing fabric. This is the fabric that your design will go on. Your backing fabric needs to be at least 8" larger in width and in depth than your pattern to leave a 4" margin on each side.

Your backing fabric needs to have an open weave that will allow the hook to pass through the hole. Many years ago grain was bought in large burlap sacks. Thrifty New Englanders used these sacks as the backing for their rugs. Over time it was found that burlap sacking doesn't last and begins to break down over time. Today there are much better fabrics to use as backing.

Left to right: Burlap, linen, monk's cloth.

Sometimes you hear the terms "weft" and "warp." Let me explain the difference. Weft (sometimes called "woof") are threads which run from selvage edge to selvage edge. (The selvage consists of the "bound" edges that don't unravel.) Warp are the lengthwise threads.

Scottish burlap (not to be confused with Angus [sack] burlap) is an oil-treated, evenly woven mesh. It tends to be a little rough when hooking and sheds small fibers, which can become a little annoying. This is the least expensive of the backings. Do not purchase Angus burlap, which is more commonly found in stores. This burlap does not have an even weave, is very rough, and is used for wrapping the root balls of trees.

Scottish burlap is versatile and will hold finer strips but is also great for primitive hooking with large strips.

Monk's cloth is a soft but heavy 100% cotton cloth. It usually has a white grid every 2", which will help keep your lines straighter. The size of the holes is very important. Buy cloth that has 12 holes per inch (12 count). Anything less and your strips/yarn will not stay in. The 7 count monk's cloth is for afghans.

Monk's cloth comes in sizes up to 72" and 144" and is a moderately priced backing. It works well with both narrow and wide strips.

Linen is very strong and easy to work on. It is usually the most expensive. A very pliant foundation, it will also last forever. The mesh opening is suitable for wool strips from 5/32" to 3/8" wide.

Rug Warp is a heavier cotton backing with a tighter weave, very good for thin strips. The warp and weft threads are rounded so your wool strips/yarn are not "scraping" against the thread as you pull it through.

Try each one and decide which is best for you.

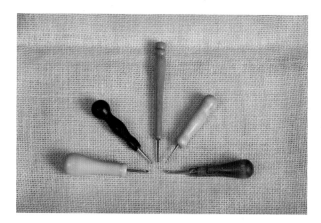

Variety of hook sizes with various handles.

Rug Hooking Tool

Rug hooking tools come in different sizes with different handles. Basically a rug hook is a crochet hook with a wooden handle. The hook ranges from fine (for thinner strips) to very coarse or primitive (for thicker strips). Start out with a medium size hook. As you progress you can try the finer size or the more primitive size hooks depending on what type of hooking you prefer.

The handles vary from bulb shape to pencil shape to a variety of ergonomically correct shapes. You'll find handles made from some very exotic wood, for a price, of course! It's a good idea to have more than one handle shape. During long hooking sessions switch between the two intermittently to prevent hand cramps.

Shank size is important too. The shank is the area between the handle and the hook. If you are working with a larger cut strip, a large shank will open up the hole for you to pull the loop through.

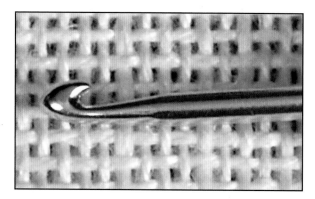

Close up of hook end.

Hooking Material

Yarn

Wool yarn is my favorite hooking material. It's what I first started with and still love. It's easy to dye, although it readily comes in many colors. It's a nice long length so there's not a lot of stopping and starting and it's ready to go once you wind the skein into a ball. When choosing wool yarn, look for bulky or worsted weight. For projects that are not going to be walked on, the new specialty yarns can add some pizzazz to areas of your project.

An assortment of yarns and wools.

Wool Fabric

Wool fabric is the most commonly used fabric. New wool off the bolt is wonderful, but a less expensive source of wool is old clothes. A great source for old clothes are thrift shops and yard sales. When looking for wool clothing, look for 100% wool, medium weight not light weight or winter coat weight. Do not use gabardine, which unravels easily. When you get home, immediately put the clothes in your washer with hot water and a little liquid detergent. Unfortunately, you don't know what kind of insects might have gotten into the clothes. If you can't wash them right away, put the clothing into a garbage bag with mothballs until you are able to wash it.

Wherever you have gotten your wool, the preparation is the same. All wool needs to shrink to keep it from unraveling. Wash the wool in your washing machine on a hot setting with a little detergent. Wash the same colors together. Rinse with cold water. When the cycle is finished, toss the wool in the dryer and dry until it is slightly damp. Do not over dry.

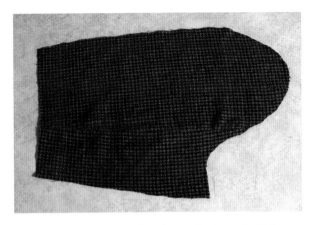

Deconstruct wool clothing found at yard sales or thrift shops.

Frames and Hoops

The frame or hoop will keep the backing taut while you hook. This is necessary for nice, even loops. If you're not sure about rug hooking as a hobby, start out with a large quilting hoop. This is much less expensive and works well with monk's cloth.

Rug hooking frames are usually rectangular with gripper strips on all sides. I have a sit-on rug frame, which I love. It swivels easily and let's me get comfortable when I hook. If you're in the market for a rug hooking frame, search the Internet for all different varieties.

Wools of different textures.

Gripper frame and quilting hoop.

Other Supplies

Red Dot Tracer – Red Dot Tracer is a non-woven tracing material with red dots marking each square inch. The red dots help you keep your patterns straight. This material is thin enough for a marker to go through onto your backing fabric. You'll find it at most fabric stores.

Permanent Marker – You will need a permanent maker such as Sharpie® Fine Point. Have two different colors of markers. If you make a mistake as you are drawing your pattern onto your backing make the correction in a **different color marker**.

Scissors – A sharp pair of scissors are necessary for cutting your tails without pulling loops out. Embroidery scissors will help you lift any lower loops to the height of the other loops. Appliqué scissors lay flat on your rug to cut off tails.

Embroidery scissors lifting a loop.

Red dot tracer, embroidery scissors, appliqué scissors, black marker.

Appliqué scissors lay flat for cutting tails.

Techniques

Dyeing and Over-dyeing Your Wool Fabric or Yarn

As I have said before, when I began hooking I began with wool yarn. I lived close to a store that stocked wool yarn in many different colors. What more did I need? But a friend of mine was using wool strips. "Not me, no way, I'll never use wool fabric." I now buy wool by the bolt. When I read about dyeing wool, I again said, "Not me, no way, I'll never dye wool." I now love to dye wool. The great thing is – the more mottled the color comes out, the better, so you don't have to be great at dyeing. The mottled color gives the rug so much character and personality, giving you a lot of leeway. Plus, if you get a color you don't like you can over-dye it and change its personality completely.

There are several places to get dye for rug hooking. See Resources at the end of this book. Read the instructions for the dye that you purchase. The following are general directions.

Samples of mottled wool.

Equipment for Dyeing

The equipment you use for dyeing should NEVER be used for food!
A large enamel or stainless steel pot
Glass measuring cup
Dye
White vinegar
Measuring spoons
Long handled tongs for stirring and flipping
Apron
Rubber gloves

Dyeing equipment.

Wool yarn ready for dyeing.

For yarn: coil into a large, loose circle, tie each quadrant with a scrap of yarn.

1.) Presoak your material by adding a little dish detergent to warm water and soak for 30 minutes. I use a gallon storage bag if I'm doing small amounts.

2.) Donning your apron and gloves, follow the directions on your dye package to dissolve dye.

3.) Fill your large pot with approximately enough water to cover your wool. Add your dye and bring the water to a boil.

4.) Slowly add your wool. Stir constantly for a more even color. Leave crumpled for a more mottled look.

5.) Add the vinegar according to the dye packet. When the water has cleared, all the dye has been absorbed.

6.) "Cook" the wool for one hour. Remove the pot from the heat.

7.) Rinse the wool first in hot water, then bringing it slowly to cool water. Alternately, you could let it cool in the pot overnight. Rinse the wool in your washing machine on the rinse setting. If you are doing yarn, place it in a hosiery bag first.

(YARN ONLY) – After removing from the washer, take your yarn into the backyard. Holding one of the tied ends, swing the yarn firmly in a circle to remove excess water. The yarn should make a "whizzing" sound as you swing it. From there you can either line dry the yarn or put it in a lingerie bag and use your dryer. If using the dryer, check every ten minutes to make sure the yarn doesn't overdry.

8.) Dry in your dryer on medium heat. Add a towel or two to the dryer so that the wool moves around. Small pieces tend to cling to the drum, which can cause wrinkling.

There are many books available on dyeing wool. Check with your local library or online for books and recipes for dyes.

Cutting the Wool

In general you need approximately five times as much wool as the area that you are hooking. How you hook will determine if you need more or less. How high are your hoops? How close are your rows?

If you are doing, say, a sky or any type of large background, use several slightly different shades of a color. Cut several strips of each and

mix them up, blindly pull from your pile. This adds character to your piece, giving it a nice mottled background.

In order to hook the wool we will need strips – many, many strips. But don't get ahead of yourself; you want to cut as you go. Wool is valuable and if you have cut a pile of 4/32" but then decide an area would look better in a 6/32" you may not have enough wool to be able to recut more for your project.

Strips are cut into 32nds of an inch up to 8. If the instructions call for a #6 cut the strips will be 6/32". A #8 cut is 8/32" or 1/4". There are several ways to cut the wool, but you will first need to square up your wool. Snip into your wool about 2" from the selvage edge (the edge that is woven so it won't unravel). Take each side of the snip in your hands and rip. The wool will tear on the straight of the grain. Your strips MUST be on the straight of the grain or they will be weak. Weak strips can tear when you hook them or when the finished rug is walked on.

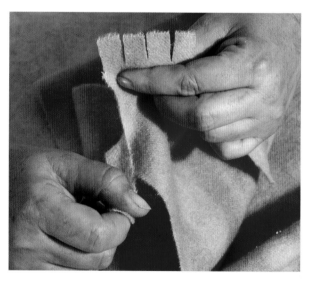

Snipping the wool in 1/2" increments and tearing.

The least expensive method is to tear all of your strips. This is great for primitive rugs that use a #8 (1/4"), #9 (3/8") or a #10 (1/2"). Just snip your fabric in the desired increments and tear away. Note: #9, and #10 do not follow the 32nd of an inch rule.

Another inexpensive way to cut wool is with a rotary cutter, a cutting mat, and a see-through acrylic ruler. Place your wool on the cutting mat and place your ruler on the appropriate fraction of an inch lined up with the torn edge of the wool. Cut several strips and flip your wool so you begin cutting from the other torn edge.

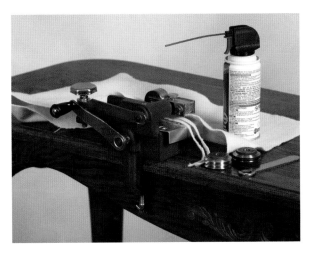

Using an acrylic ruler, cutting mat, and rotary cutter.

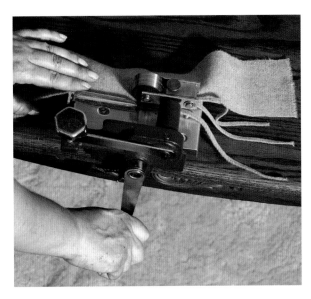

Frasier Model 500-1 clamp-on with cutter blades.

When you find that you're "hooked" on rug hooking, a little more costly but much easier way to cut wool is with a wool cutter. There are several good brands available. I use the Fraser Model 500-1. It's easy to change the cutting heads to different widths for different projects.

When changing colors on your cutter, a blast of canned air (found in stationary stores) will remove wool residue.

Very easy to use.

Cutter blades come in many different sizes.

Transferring the Pattern

First you will need the pattern to be the correct size. On a copy machine enlarge the pattern to fit your need.

To enlarge –

1.) Measure your piece diagonally from corner to corner.

2.) Measure your pattern diagonally from corner to corner.

3.) Divide the number of inches you want the pattern to be by the number of inches the pattern is.

4.) The "quotient" is the number you set the copier on to enlarge the pattern.

    i.e. desired size is 21", pattern is 17"

    $21 \div 17 = 1.23$, set the copier to 123%

To decrease –

1.) Measure your piece diagonally from corner to corner.

2.) Measure your pattern diagonally from corner to corner.

3.) Divide the number of inches the pattern measures by the number of inches you want.

4.) The "quotient" is the number you set the copier on to decrease the pattern.

    i.e. desired size is 17", pattern is 21"

    $17 \div 21 = .82$, set the copier to 82%

To enlarge something as large as a rug you will have to enlarge the pattern in sections and then piece the pattern together. If your copier will not enlarge large enough, you may have to take the pattern to a copy shop.

Once you have the pattern to the correct size, tape it to a flat surface such as a table or a hard floor. Place the Red Dot Tracer on top of the pattern and tape or pin the Tracer securely. Make sure the red dots line up on any straight lines in the pattern. With the marker, trace all the lines of the pattern onto the Red Dot Tracer.

Now tape your backing fabric to the table. Lay the Red Dot Tracer pattern on the backing fabric, leaving approximately 4" on each side for the hoop or frame. Make sure the straight lines of your pattern follow the straight lines of your fabric grain. Tape or pin securely. I use a lot of long hatpins.

Trace your pattern on to the red dot tracer.

Trace over the pattern slowly so the marker flows through the tracer and onto your backing fabric. Lift a corner of the tracer and make sure your lines are visible. Go over any that are not visible. Use a ruler for straight lines. If your pattern is too light when you remove the Red Dot, just go over the lines with your marker.

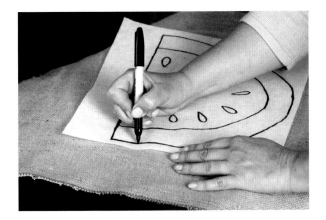

Place the red dot tracer onto your fabric and go over your lines slowly with a marker.

Another way to trace your pattern onto the backing is with a light box tracer. These are small rectangular acrylic boxes with a light bulb inside. This method is good for smaller projects – pillows, stocking, or eye mask. Light boxes can be found at craft or art supply stores and are relatively inexpensive. I find I use mine a lot.

Tape your pattern to the light box, place your backing fabric over the pattern and secure. Trace with the black marker.

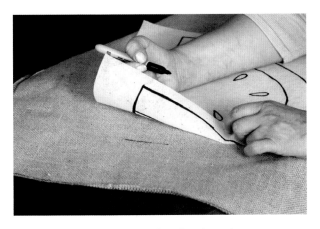

Lift to make sure the marker is going through.

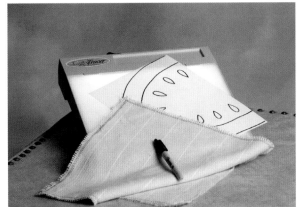

A light box for tracing on the pattern.

Darken your markings if necessary.

Using the light box.

Finishing the Edges to Prevent Unraveling

Once your pattern is traced on, you will need to prevent the backing from unraveling. You can either zigzag stitch around the edge if you own a sewing machine or hand stitch two rows close together with a 1/4" straight stitch. If you're lucky enough to have use of a serger, serge the edges.

Flip fabric over with sticky side of tape facing up.

Taping, serging, and zigzag stitching to prevent unraveling.

No sewing machine? Another way to finish the edges is with 2" tape – masking, painters or duct. Place 1" on your edge and fold the other inch to the back.

NOTE: Before you start hooking, you must decide how you are going to finish the binding of your rug. For the binding tape method you will want to attach the binding tape before you start hooking. (See Finishing Your Rug on page 20.)

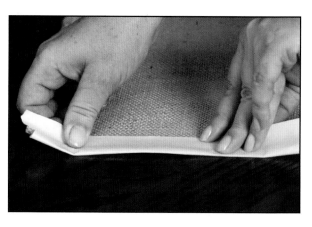

Fold tape over and smooth to secure.

Place 1" of tape on the edge of your fabric.

Hooking

Place the center of your project on the center of your frame or hoop. Gently pull the fabric side-to-side and top to bottom so that it is taut and straight. You are going to hook from the center out.

Center your design on your frame.

Stretch your fabric so that it is taut.

1.) With the hook in your dominant hand and the yarn/strip underneath the backing fabric, stick the hook through a hole, wrap the yarn or wool strip around the hook, and pull up the yarn or wool strip through the hole about 1" above the fabric. Keep the yarn/strip in your other hand under the fabric. The first time you are just bringing up the tail.

Lifting up the first tail.

The hook catches the wool strip underneath the backing fabric.

2.) Stick the hook into the second hole and repeat to make a loop. The loop should be about 1/4" high off your fabric. The "rule" is the height of the loop is the same as the width of the strip. If it is more than this, give a little tug with your left hand to bring it down to the right height. The underside of the loop should be snug against your backing fabric.

Bringing up the first loop.

3.) When picking the next hole to stick your hook into, you want your loops to be touching each other but not crushing each other. Skip to the second or third hole for the next loop. If your loops are drooping over, they are too close. Keep hooking until you need to change color. Pull that final loop up higher than the others and cut the loop leaving a tail on top and pulling the rest of the strip out from the bottom. If you run out of a strip, pull the final bit on top to make a tail. Your next color (or the same color if you ran out) will start in the **same** hole that your last one left off. Two tails will come out of one hole on top of your project.

Hook just inside the black drawn line, unless the instructions say otherwise. Outline an area first and fill in. The projects in this book will tell you to hook on the line in a particular color. This is to define an area. (Example: poinsettia on French Horn Christmas Stocking on page 57.)

Bringing up the next loop.

Make sure your non-hooking hand is keeping the strip straight underneath the backing. You don't want any twisted loops on top or bottom. Twists or lumps on the bottom will loosen the individual threads of the strip as the rug is walked on and the rug will start to wear in that area.

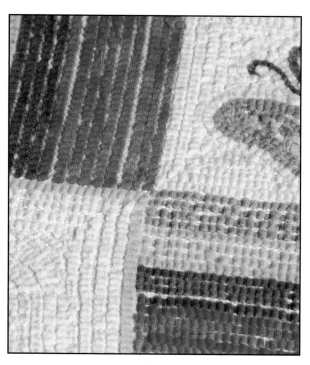
The back should be smooth and neat.

Hooking Backgrounds

As you finish a motif, hook one or two rows of background around it. As you begin the background, start with the edges first and hook the outline of your project. This will ensure that you stay on the grain and your project is straight. After that you can hook from side to side, follow the hills or grass lines or "meander."

Hook several rows of background around a motif.

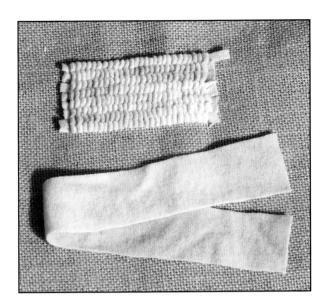

Mottled fabric hooked side to side makes a nice sky.

"Meandering" is filling in the background with swirls and spirals. If you are a beginner, draw on the swirls and spirals randomly with the black marker. With one color hook right on the spiral you have drawn. If you are using more than one color (Sheep with Watermelon on page 62), outline your spiral with a second color. You can continue with a third color or repeat with your first color. You can also "meander" with a single color. This looks especially nice with a mottled piece of wool (sky in Stay the Course on page 51).

Meandering with mottled wool.

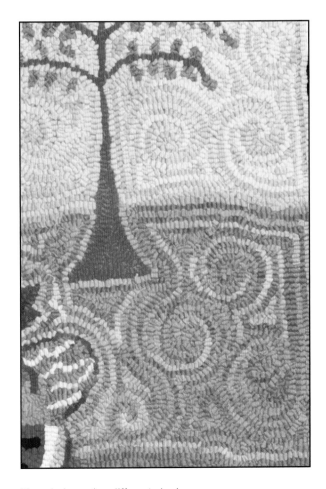

Meandering using different shades.

How do the loops stay in place? The loops stay secure because the warp and weft threads of the backing fabric shift from the yarn/wool strip and hug the loops into place. Too few loops and you will be able to see your backing material from the top, too many loops and your rug will curl like a bad perm.

Blocking Your Rug

When you are finished hooking your rug, remove it from the hoop and lay it flat. If it has become out of shape, gently tug it back into shape.

Blocking your rug.

Place your rug on an ironing board hooked side up, cover with a damp towel, and place a hot iron on the towel. Don't iron back and forth but hold the iron in one section and count to ten. Repeat all over the front of the rug. Flip the rug over and repeat on the back. Let the rug completely dry (usually twenty-four hours) before finishing the edges.

Finishing Your Rug

There are several methods to finish the binding of your rug.

Self-Hemming
1.) Zigzag your rug 3" from the hooking and cut away excess backing fabric.
2.) Working from the back, fold the zigzagged edge into the hooking.
3.) Fold the backing over to back of the rug and blind stitch flat. Make sure your thread goes through the backing fabric.

Zigzag your fabric 3" from the hooking and cut away excess fabric.

Fold the zigzagged edge to the hooked edge.

Fold the backing over to the back of the rug.

Whipstitch flat.

Binding Tape – Add the binding tape before hooking the rug.

Binding tape is a 1 1/4" cotton twill that comes in many colors to match your rug. It is available in specialty stores and on the Internet. (*See Resources*.) You must preshrink the binding by washing in hot water and drying before using it.

1.) Measure the four sides of your rug and add 10" for your binding length. Start away from a corner and place the binding right sides together on the outside of your border line. Sew by hand or by machine with a heavy-duty thread.

2.) Now hook the rug.

3.) When you have finished your hooking, fold the binding to the back. To miter the corners, pull the corner in first. Next fold in the side you have been working on, then fold in the side you have to do

4.) With heavy-duty thread whipstitch the binding to the backing. Make sure you go through the backing fabric.

Fold the binding to the back.

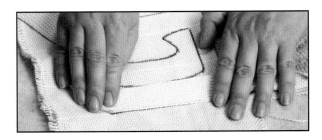

Binding tape sewn to unhooked design.

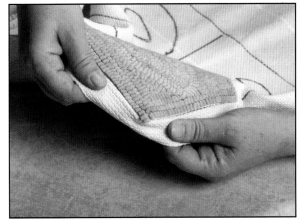

Push the corner loops out.

Cut away excess backing fabric.

Miter the corners and sew flat.

Whipstitching with cording.

1.) Mark your backing fabric to 1" from the last row of hooking and zigzag on this line twice around. Cut away excess backing. Angle the cuts on the corners.

2.) The cording should be as thick as your rug. Place the rug right side down on a table and place the cording on the outside edge of your hooking.

3.) Flip the rug right side up. Thread a large eyed needle (#16 needlepoint needle) with an 18-24" length of tapestry or wool yarn. Starting in an area that is not on a corner, insert the needle through the back along the hooked edge, pull the yarn through, leaving a 2" tail, pull the yarn to the back, and insert the needle right next to your first stitch, catching your tail. You want your first two inches of stitches to cover the tail. When you run out of yarn, feed your needle under the already stitched area, bring the needle up and cut off any excess close to the whipstitching.

4.) Continue until you reach the corner. When you reach the corner, continue around the edge. You will not have a crisp corner but a slightly rounded one.

Bring the needle over and to the back and stick it in close to the first stitch.

Pull the yarn reasonably taut for an even finish.

Lay the yarn tail along the cording.

Keep your whip stitching close together.

Stick your needle in from the back as close to the hooking as you can.

To end the yarn, run it back through your previous whip stitching.

Wool with cording – When purchasing your wool, buy extra for your edging.

1.) Mark your backing fabric to 1" from last row of hooking. Zigzag on this line and cut away excess backing.

2.) Measure around your rug and added approximately 6". Cut a strip of wool approximately 2 1/2" to 3" in width and the length of your rug plus the 6". It's not necessary to cut on the bias but it will make it easier to go around the corners. You may need to piece together several pieces. Join pieces at right angles. This reduces bulk.

Iron seam flat.

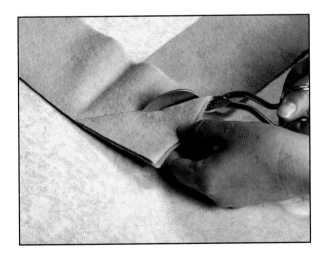

To make a wool strip longer, put two strips of fabric at right angles and sew from corner to corner.

3.) On your long wool strip place the cording slightly to the right of center. Fold the left side over the cording. Using the zipper or cording foot on your sewing machine, sew along the edge of the cording as close as you can. Sew the entire length of the strip with matching thread.

Cut away the corner piece.

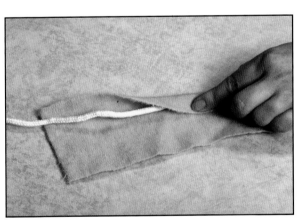

Place the cording slightly to the right of center.

4.) On the front side of the rug, place the stitching line of the wool strip right up against the last row of hooking, leaving the long side free. Sew by hand starting about 1" from the edge of the cording. You don't want to see any backing material peeking through on the front.

5.) When the two edges meet, cut away any excess cording. Fold the raw edge under of the piece that will lie on top.

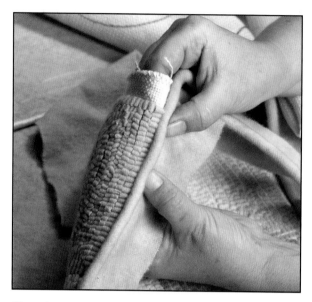

Place the cording against the last hooked row.

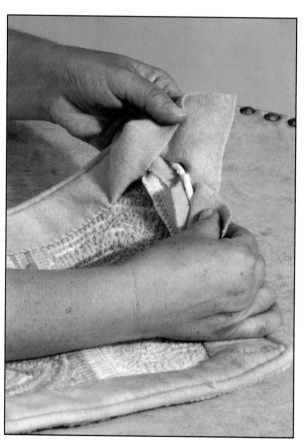

Cut the cording so the ends butt.

Sew by hand keeping the cording seam as close to the hooking as possible.

6.) Fold the raw edge under of the piece that will lie on top. Fold the raw edge under and whipstitch for a neater look.

Lay the folded edge over the raw edge.

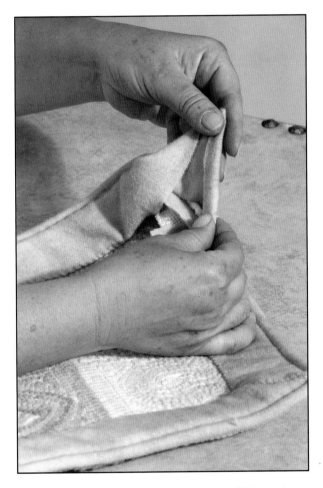

Fold the raw edge under of the piece that will lay on top.

7) Miter the corners folding one edge flat and folding the corner of the other edge on the diagonal. Whip stitch to secure.

8.) Iron once again following the directions for blocking.

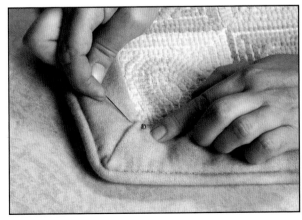

Whipstitch the raw edge under for a nice finish.

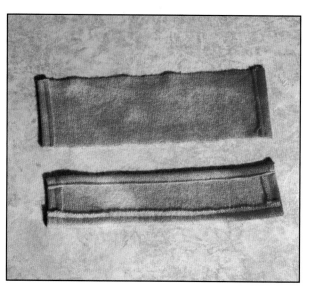

Blind stitch the non-slip mat to the bottom of your rug.

A word on latex backing. My word is NO! I don't believe in using latex backing. As I was doing research for this book I came across several people and websites that suggest it. When you apply latex to the back of your rug you are doing several things: 1.) Preventing air circulation; 2.) Allowing dirt and sand to stay trapped and grind your wool fibers; and 3.) Making it almost impossible to repair any pulls if they should occur. If you have hooked correctly your loops will stay in. To prevent slipping, use a rubber no-slip pad under your rug. You can sew this right to your rug. All of the rugs in my house have no-slip padding sewn on and then they are taped to the floor with a no-slip carpet tape. It peels from the floor when you want to change rugs and leaves no residue.

Never tack your rug directly onto the wall. The weight of the wool will pull the corners down and you will damage the rug. The weight needs to be evenly distributed along the top of the rug.

To make your rug into a wall hanging, add a sleeve to the back with muslin so that a dowel or rod can be inserted. Cut a piece of wool or fabric the width of your project and 4-5" in length. Turn in the sides 1/2" and sew flat, turn the top and bottom under 1/2", and sew flat. Whipstitch the sleeve 1" from the top of the back of your project.

Rugs also look wonderful framed. Cut a piece of mdf (medium density fiberboard, available at lumberyards) to the finished size of your rug. Place the hooking face down on a table, place the mdf on top and staple or tack the excess fabric to the board. Bring this to a frame shop for framing.

Turn sides under 1/2" and sew. Turn top and bottom under 1/2" and sew.

Blind stitch the sleeve to the top of your project and insert a dowel.

The Final Touch

You know that years from now you will never remember when you made your rug or why. On muslin record your name, the date, and if there is space write a few lines – why you made this rug or who you made it for. If you made it as a gift, write the care and cleaning instructions on the label. Write everything with a fine permanent marker. Turn under the edges and blind stitch to the back of your rug.

Care and Cleaning of Your Rug

Your beautiful rug is on the floor and your golden retriever likes to sleep on it. How do you remove the dog hair? Some books and websites will tell you not to vacuum. I personally have had no problems vacuuming my rugs. If you choose to vacuum, use a vacuum without a beater roller or brush attachment.

For spills, blot immediately and use a damp cloth with Ivory soap gently on that area. Place that area under the faucet and let the stream of water rinse the soap out. Blot dry with a terry cloth towel. Let dry completely before putting it back on the floor to avoid mildew.

When storing rugs, roll them with the hooked side out.

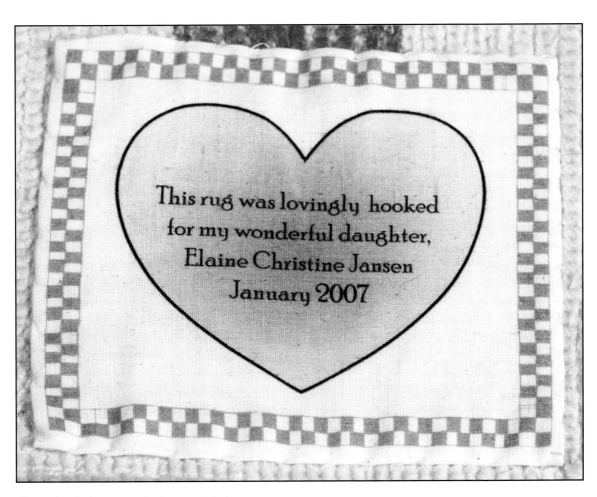

Computer design on muslin for a rug label.

Projects

"It's your garden!" My good friend, Dinah, uses that phrase when it comes to color and design. The projects in this book are to give you a jumping off point to rug hooking. Feel free to change the colors to suit your décor. It's your garden! Turquoise flowers, green skies, red sheep. These are *your* projects. Enlarge or reduce the sizes if you have a specific area of your floor, stool or wall in mind.

For each project you can use either wool strips or yarn, whichever you prefer. To figure out the amount of yarn – 1 oz. of yarn will cover a 4" x 4" area.

Before you begin these projects read the Supplies and Techniques sections of this book. Materials such as the hook, red dot tracer, scissors, and other basic supplies are not listed individually. All yardage is based on a 60" width.

Americana Stair Treads

Stair treads are quick, easy, and very functional. If something happens to one, you just lift up that tread and repair it or replace it with a newly hooked one. It's important to secure them to the stair so there are no slipping accidents.

Liberty Stair Tread

Finished size: 25 1/2" x 8"
#8 cut

Wool:
 3/8 yard blue
 1/3 yard gold
 7" x 7" red

Materials:
 33" x 16" backing fabric
 2 oz. blue tapestry or wool
yarn for binding

1.) Enlarge the pattern and transfer onto your backing fabric. Refer to "Transferring Your Pattern" on page 14. Finish the edges referring to "Finishing the Edges to Prevent Unraveling" on page 20.

2.) Hook in the following order:
 "Liberty" – gold
 Star and letter inserts – red
 background – blue

3.) Block your rug following "Blocking Your Rug" on page 20.

4.) Finish the rug following "Whipstitching with cording" on page 20 or any of the other options in the "Finishing Your Rug" section on page 20.

5.) Block again following "Blocking Your Rug" on page 20.

Stair treads must be firmly secured to the stair with nails or strong adhesive.

Stars and Stripes Stair Tread

Finished size: 25 1/2" x 8"
#8 cut

Wool:
  1/4 yard red
  1/8 yard gold
  1/8 yard blue
  1/8 yard off white

Materials:
  33" x 16" backing fabric
  1 oz. blue tapestry or wool yarn
  1 oz. red tapestry or wool yarn

1.) Enlarge the pattern and transfer onto your backing fabric. Refer to "Transferring Your Pattern" on page 14. Finish the edges, referring to "Finishing the Edges to Prevent Unraveling" on page 20.
  2.) Hook in the following order:
    star – gold
    square – blue
    top and bottom stripe – red
    middle stripe – off white

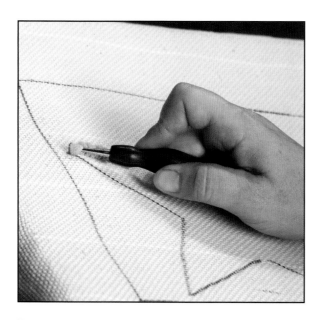

Turn the loop on the point to change direction.

When reaching a point, twist the loop around to face the direction you want to go in. This will keep the wool from twisting underneath.

3.) Block your rug following "Blocking Your Rug" on page 20.

4.) Finish the rug following "Whipstitching with cording" on page 20 or any of the other options in the "Finishing Your Rug" section.

5.) Block again following "Blocking Your Rug" on page 20.

Stair treads must be firmly secured to the stairs with nails or strong adhesive.

Hook the stripes in a row to the end, then hook up the side with the appropriate color.

America

Finished size: 25 1/2" x 8"
#8 cut

Wool:
    3/8 yard blue
    1/3 yard red
    1/16 yard gold

Materials:
    33" x 16" backing fabric
    2 oz. blue tapestry or wool yarn
for binding

1.) Enlarge the pattern and transfer onto your backing fabric. Refer to "Transferring Your Pattern" on page 14. Finish the edges, referring to "Finishing the Edges to Prevent Unraveling" on page 16.

2.) Hook in the following order:
    "America" – red
    Shadow – gold
    background – blue

3.) Block your rug following "Blocking Your Rug" on page 20.

4.) Finish the rug following "Whipstitching with cording" on page 20 or any of the other options in the "Finishing Your Rug" section on page 20.

5.) Block again following "Blocking Your Rug" on page 20.

Stair treads must be firmly secured to the stairs with nails or strong adhesive.

Red, White, and Blue With Stars

Finished size: 25 1/2" x 8"
#8 cut

Wool:
   1/2 yard gold
   12" x 16" red
   12" x 16" white
   12" x 16" blue

Materials:
   33" x 16" backing fabric
   1 oz. red tapestry or wool yarn for binding
   1 oz. white tapestry or wool yarn for binding
   1 oz. blue tapestry or wool yarn for binding

1.) Enlarge the pattern and transfer onto your backing fabric. Refer to "Transferring Your Pattern" on page 14. Finish the edges referring to "Finishing the Edges to Prevent Unraveling" on page 16.

2.) Hook as follows:
   Stars – gold
   Left square background – red
   Middle square background – white
   Right square background – blue

3.) Block your rug following "Blocking Your Rug" on page 20.

4.) Finish the rug following "Whipstitching with cording" on page 20 or any of the other options in the "Finishing Your Rug" section on page 20.

5.) Block again following "Blocking Your Rug" on page 20.

Stair treads need to be firmly secured to the stairs with nails or strong adhesive.

With a Song in My Heart Footstool

Finished size: 10" x 10"
#6 cut

If you can't find a square stool, extend the branches and adjust the flowers and cherries to fit your space.

When doing small dots such as the eye and the highlight in the cherries do three hooks of the color. Hook once to bring up the tail, move over 1 hole and hook a loop, move over one hole and hook once more and cut off, leaving a tail in the third hole.

Wool:

1/4 yard light blue
12" x 9" yellow (gold)
12" x 6" brown
12" x 4" dark blue
10" x 6" dark purple
10" x 6" light purple
10" x 5" light green
10" x 5" dark green
10" x 5" red

Materials:

18" x 18" backing fabric
light blue wool or tapestry yarn
50" medium cording

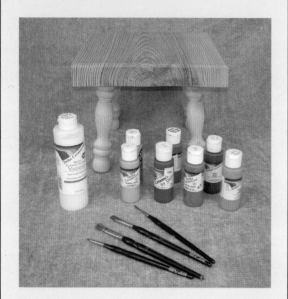

Unfinished stool and supplies.

For the stool

10" x 10" footstool with decorative legs
sealer
fine sandpaper
paintbrushes

Delta Ceramcoat 2 oz. Paints:

Antique Gold
Blue Heaven
GP Purple
Liberty Blue
Medium Foliage Green
Passion
Tompte Red
Delta matte varnish

1.) Enlarge the pattern and transfer onto your backing fabric. Refer to "Transferring Your Pattern" on page 14. Finish the edges, referring to "Finishing the Edges to Prevent Unraveling" on page 16. Your pattern should be 1/2" smaller on each side. The cording will add back the 1/2".

Hook the branches with brown, two rows of loops for the main branch and one row of loops for the offshoots. Hook around the outside edge with Light Blue.

Hook the bird's body with dark blue. His wing, tail, and beak are gold. His eye is black.

2.) Outline the left side of the leaves with the dark green. The inside is light green. The flowers are gold for the centers. The outer circle of each petal is dark purple; the inside is light purple. The cherries are red with a highlight of gold. The tendrils are one each of light purple, red, and gold.

3.) Fill in the background with the light blue.

Finished hooked pad.

4.) Block following directions on page xxx. Stitch 1" from the design with two rows of zigzag stitches and trim away excess backing fabric. Measure the outside edge and add 3". Cut the measured length of cording. Whipstitch the cording with the light blue tapestry yarn following the directions on page 20.

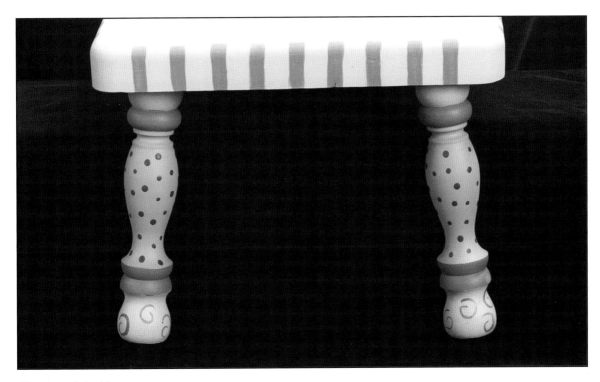

Close up of stool legs.

5.) Seal the stool following the directions on the sealer. Sand the stool with the sandpaper. Paint the stool top Blue Heaven. The legs are from top to bottom: GP Purple, Medium Foliage Green, Antique Gold, Medium Foliage Green, and GP Purple.

6.) With the back of your brush make Tompte Red dots on the Antique Gold, redippping your brush after every two dots. With the Passion make swirls on the GP Purple.

7.) Seal the stool with Delta matte varnish.

You can permanently glue the rug to the top of the stool or use hook and loop tape to secure it.

Peace Rug

Finished size: 40" x 26 1/2"
#8 cut
Butterfly corners #6 cut

Wool:
1 1/2 yard yellow
5/8 yard lime green
1/2 yard hot pink
1/2 yard orange
1/2 yard aqua
1/2 yard purple

Materials:
48" x 34" backing fabric
4 oz. lime green tapestry or wool yarn for binding

1.) Enlarge the pattern and transfer onto your backing fabric. The lines are easier to do with a ruler. Refer to "Transferring Your Pattern" on page 14. Finish the edges referring to "Finishing the Edges to Prevent Unraveling" on page 16.

2.) As you do each letter hook several rows around it with yellow background as you go.

Close up of the letters.

Hook as follows:
- "P" – hot pink
- "E" – orange
- "A" – aqua
- "C" – lime green
- "E" – purple.

Finish hooking the background with yellow.

3.) Hook the inner border with lime green.

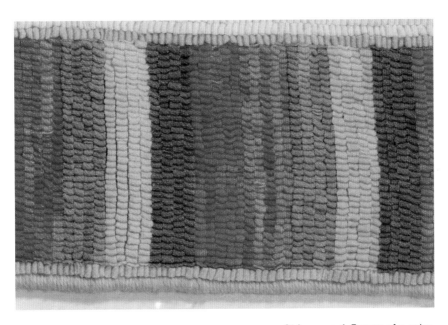

Stripes are 4-5 rows of a color.

4.) Hook the striped border in the same color order as the letters (hot pink, orange, aqua, lime green and purple).

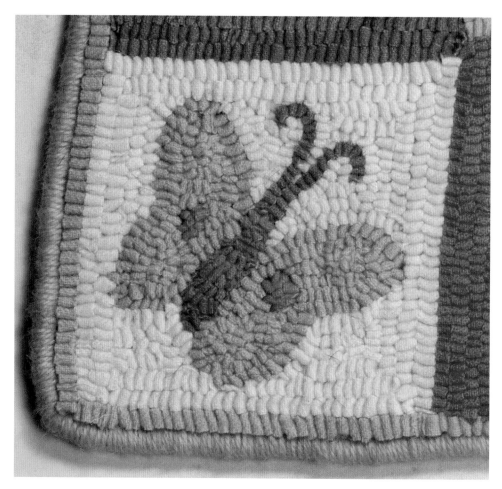

Butterflies are a #6 cut for more detail.

5.) The butterflies are done in a #6 cut for more detail. Hook as follows:

> body with pink and purple
> antenna are purple
> spots are lime green and orange
> wings are aqua
> Hook the background with yellow.

6.) Hook the outer border with lime green.

7.) Block your rug following "Blocking Your Rug" on page 20.

8.) Finish the rug following "Whipstitching with cording" on page 20 or any of the other options in the Finishing Your Rug section.

9.) Block again following "Blocking Your Rug" on page 20.

My little girl, Dooney, with pillows and rug.

For these pillow projects, find your material first, then find or dye your wool to coordinate. The pillows look great in pastels or bright colors.

Look for funky trims and embellishments at your local sewing and craft stores. All kinds of things could be used on these cool pillows – maybe a pink feather boa, braided cording, oversized buttons or beaded trim.

Play Pillow

Finished size: 15" x 15" Finished hooked design is 12" x 4 1/2"
#6 cut

Wool:

    1/8 yard hot pink
    12" x 14" lime green

Materials:

    20" x 12 1/2" backing fabric
    15" x 15" pillow form (or fiberfill for stuffing)
    1/2 yard colorful fabric
    2 yards coordinating ribbon or trim
    coordinating sewing thread

1.) With a permanent maker draw a rectangle 12" x 4 1/2" on your backing fabric, making sure you are on the straight of the grain. Enlarge the pattern and transfer onto your backing fabric. Refer to "Transferring Your Pattern" on page 14. Finish the edges referring to "Finishing the Edges to Prevent Unraveling" on page 16.

2.) Hook the lettering with lime green. Hook the background with hot pink.

3.) Block your finished design following the directions on page 20.

4.) Zigzag 1" from the hooked design and cut away excess backing. Pull unhooked backing edges to the back and secure by sewing or using iron-on hemming tape.

5.) Cut the fabric into (2) 16" x 16" pieces. Center the hooked design on one piece of fabric and whipstitch into place.

6.) Cut the ribbon into (4) 16" pieces. Place one piece along the top edge of the hooked design and pin in place; place a second piece along the bottom edge of the hooked design and pin in place. Sew along each edge of the ribbon to secure. Place another piece of the ribbon along the left side of the hooked design and pin in place, lace the last piece of the ribbon along the right side of the hooked design and pin in place. Sew along each edge of the ribbon to secure.

7.) Place right sides of fabric together and stitch using a 1/2" seam allowance. Leave an 8" opening at the bottom to insert the pillow form. (Leave a smaller opening if you are using the fiberfill.) Trim excess fabric. Turn the pillow inside out. Push out the corners.

8.) Insert the pillow form or fiberfill and whipstitch the opening closed.

Dream Pillow

Finished size: 21" x 12" Finished hooked size: 15" x 4 1/2"
#6 cut

Wool:
    1/8 yard yellow
    6" x 6" purple
    6" x 6" lime green
    6" x 6" aqua
    6" x 6" orange
    6" x 6" hot pink

Materials:
    23" x 12" backing fabric
    1/3 yard colorful fabric
    45" orange trim
    45" aqua trim
    4 coordinating silk flowers
    12" x 21" pillow form (or fiberfill for stuffing)
    Orange sewing thread
    Aqua sewing thread

1.) With a permanent marker, draw a rectangle 15" x 4 1/2" on your backing fabric, making sure you are on the straight of the grain. Enlarge the pattern and transfer onto your backing fabric. Refer to "Transferring Your Pattern" on page 14. Finish the edges referring to "Finishing the Edges to Prevent Unraveling" on page 16.

2.) Hook as follows:
    "D" hot pink
    "R" orange
    "E" aqua
    "A" lime green
    "M" purple
    The background is hooked in yellow.

3.) Block your finished design following the directions on page 20.

4.) Zigzag 1" from hooked design and cut away excess. Pull unhooked backing edges to the back and secure by sewing or using iron on hemming tape.

5.) Cut the fabric into (2) 13" x 22" pieces. Center the hooked design on one piece of fabric and whipstitch into place.

6.) Butt the orange trim against the hooked design and zigzag stitch with orange thread to secure. Repeat with the aqua trim and aqua thread. Sew a flower to each corner.

7.) Place right sides of fabric together and stitch using a 1/2" seam allowance. Leave an 8" opening at the bottom to insert the pillow form. (Leave a smaller opening if you are using the fiberfill.) Trim excess fabric. Turn the pillow inside out. Push out the corners.

8.) Insert pillow form or fiberfill and whipstitch the opening closed.

Love Pillow

Finished size: 16" x 16" Finished hooked size: 10" x 10"
Cut #6

Wool:
  1/8 yard hot pink
  1/8 yard aqua
  1/8 yard lime green
  1/8 yard yellow

Materials:
  18" x 18" backing fabric
  1 yard colorful fabric
  16" x 16" pillow form (or fiber-fill for stuffing)
  Pink wire cording
  Yellow wire cording
  Pink sewing thread
  Yellow sewing thread

1.) With a permanent marker, draw a 10" x 10" square on backing fabric, making sure you are on the straight of the grain. Each square will be 5" x 5". Enlarge the pattern and transfer onto your backing fabric. Refer to "Transferring Your Pattern." Finish the edges, referring to "Finishing the Edges to Prevent Unraveling" on page 16.

2.) Hook the "L" yellow, hook the background aqua. Hook the heart-shaped "O" hot pink, hook the background lime green. Hook the "V" lime green, hook the background hot pink. Hook the "E" aqua, hook the background yellow.

3.) Block your finished design following the directions on page 20.

4.) Zigzag 1" from hooked design and cut away excess. Pull unhooked backing edges to the back and secure by sewing or using iron on hemming tape.

5.) Cut the fabric into (2) 17" x 17" pieces. Center the hooked design on one piece of fabric and whipstitch into place. Butt the pink trim against the hooked design and zigzag stitch to secure. Repeat with the yellow trim.

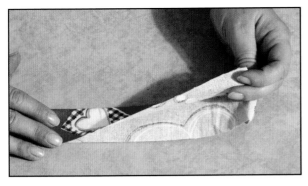

Fold the strip in half lengthwise.

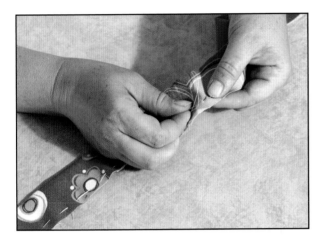

Loose running stitch.

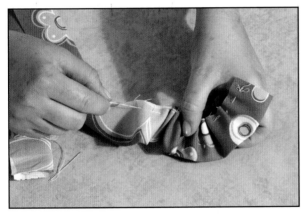

Pull the thread to make the ruffle.

Lay the edge of the ruffle on the edge of the pillow.

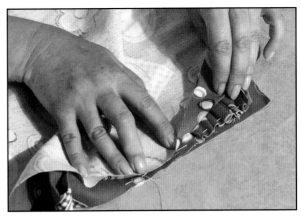

Lay the pillow bottom on top, right sides together.

Sew with a 1/2" seam allowance.

6.) To make the ruffle – cut a strip of fabric 6" x 2 yards. a.) Fold in half lengthwise and iron flat. With a loose running stitch, stitch along the open edge, gathering both thicknesses of fabric. Pull the thread slowly, making the ruffle, easing the thread gently. Lay the ruffle on the back pillow fabric with the sewn edge against the pillow edge (ruffle facing in). Pin securely, adjusting the gathers so the fullness is distributed evenly.

7.) Place the hooked pillow side face down on the pillow back so that right sides are together with the ruffle sandwiched in between. Stitch using a 1/2" seam allowance. Leave an 8" opening at the bottom to insert the pillow form. (Leave a smaller opening if you are using the fiberfill.) Trim excess fabric. Turn the pillow inside out. Push out the corners.

8.) Insert pillow form or fiberfill and whipstitch the opening closed.

Williamsburg Hooked Rug

A wonderful trip to Williamsburg, Virginia, inspired this rug. I could spend all day wandering around, admiring historic sites and going through museums.

Finished size 24" x 35"
#6 cut

Wool:
2/3 yard dark blue
3/8 yard red
1/2 yard sky blue
1/2 yard light green
1/3 yard dark green
1/3 yard medium green
1/4 yard yellow (gold)
1/4 yard brown
1/8 yard black
12" x 12" white

Materials:
Backing fabric 32" x 43"

1.) Enlarge the pattern and transfer onto your backing fabric. Refer to "Transferring Your Pattern" on page 14. Finish the edges, referring to "Finishing the Edges to Prevent Unraveling" on page 16.

2.) Hook in the following order:

windows and roof of the center house – black

center house – dark blue
vein of falling leaves – dark green
leaves – light green
sun – yellow
trees – brown
sky – blue
sheep legs, heads, and tails – black
sheep bodies – white
hill #1 – medium green

3.) Continue hooking the following:
   windows and roof of left house – black
   left house – red
   hill #2 – dark green
   windows and roof of right house – black
   right house – yellow
   hill #3 – light green
   hill #4 – light green
   hill #5 – medium green

Close up of a tulip.

4.) For the sides – Hook a small circle at the base of each tulip with yellow. Outline the center petal and the tops of the side petals with yellow. Fill in the tulip petals with red. Hook one row of dark green for the stem. The veins of each leaf are dark green; the leaves are light green. Hook the background with dark blue.

5.) Hook the checkerboard alternating with red and yellow.

6.) Block your rug following "Blocking Your Rug" on page 20.

7.) Finish the rug following *"Self hemming"* on page 20.

Beach Tote Bag

Finished hooked size: 8" x 6"
#6 cut

Wools:
 12" x 8" tan
 12" x 12" total sky blues
 6" x 6" dark blue
 6" x 6" green

Materials:
 16" x 14" backing fabric
 Inexpensive straw tote (approx. 14" x 12" surface)
 2 medium seashells with holes drilled for stringing
 Button thread
 4 shell necklaces (available at most craft stores)

1.) Transfer the pattern onto your backing fabric. Refer to "Transferring Your Pattern." Finish the edges, referring to "Finishing the Edges to Prevent Unraveling" on page 16.

2.) When hooking the letters with centers ("a," "B," and "e"), hook the center first in the background color. Hook in the following order:
 "Life's a" – dark blue wool
 "Beach" – green
 Sky area – blue
 Sand – tan

3.) Block your finished design following the directions on page xxx.

4.) Zigzag 1" from the hooked design and cut away excess backing. Pull unhooked backing edges to the back and secure by sewing or using iron-on hemming tape.

5.) Center the hooking onto the straw tote and secure with button thread and a needle. Sew the shell necklace (open) around the hooking and along the top of the tote, sew the two medium shells on the hooking.

Stay the Course

I love the stormy sea on this rug. It's fun to do – very loose and freeform.

Finished size 27" x 19 1/2"
#8 cut

If you can't find off white, ecru, or light beige, tea stain a piece of white wool. Wet your wool before you begin. Make a very strong tea in a pot on the stove – 3-4 teabags to a quart of water. Scrunch your wool into a loose ball and submerge in the tea. The scrunching will give you a mottled color. Let the wool soak until you have a color you are happy with. Then add a little white vinegar to set the color. This also works for toning down a color that is too bright.

Wool:

3/4 yard aqua

3/8 yard total mottled or assorted sky blues

1/4 yard total ocean blues (aqua, light blue, navy blue)

1/4 yard red

1/4 yard off white (ecru or light beige)

1/6 yard mottled white (for rope)

1/16 yard total mottled browns

12" x 12" black

10" x 5" white

Materials:

35" x 28" backing fabric

2 oz. red wool or tapestry yarn for binding

1.) Enlarge and transfer the pattern onto your backing fabric. Refer to "Transferring Your Pattern." Finish the edges, referring to "Finishing the Edges to Prevent Unraveling" on page 16.

2.) Begin hooking the ship as follows:

windows – black

boat, masts, sail holders – brown

sails – ecru

flags – red

3.) Hook the sky following the directions for "Meandering" on page 19 with the light blues.

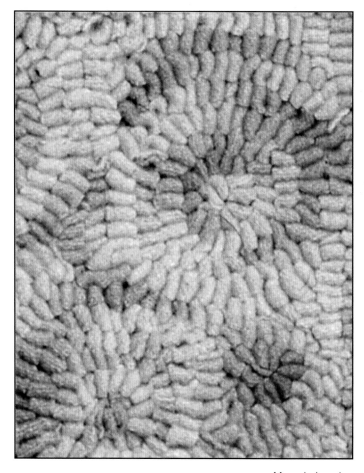

Meandering sky.

52

The stormy sea.

4.) The sea is done by hooking on the line with white. Under the white, hook with the teal. Under the teal, hook with the light blue. Under the light blue, hook with the navy. Extend some of your hooking to flow into a nearby wave. Fill in any unhooked areas with random blues.

5.) Hook the inner border with red.

6.) Hook the rope with the mottled white and black – two to three rows of white, then 1 row of black. Hook the lettering with red and highlight with mottled white. Fill in the background with turquoise.

7.) Hook the outer border with red.

8.) Block your rug following "Blocking Your Rug" on page 20.

9.) Finish the rug following "Whipstitching with cording" on page 20 or any of the other options in the Finishing Your Rug section.

10.) Block again following "Blocking Your Rug" on page 20.

Finished size: 33" diameter
#6 cut

Wool:

    5/8 yard black
    3/8 yard mottled orange/yellow
    1/4 yard yellow
    1/4 yard white
    1/4 yard red
    1/4 yard medium green
    1/4 yard dark green
    1/6 yard light green
    1/6 yard blue
    10" x 6" gold
    10" x 6" rust
    10" x 6" maroon
    10" x 6" total browns

Materials:

    2 oz. black wool or tapestry yarn for binding

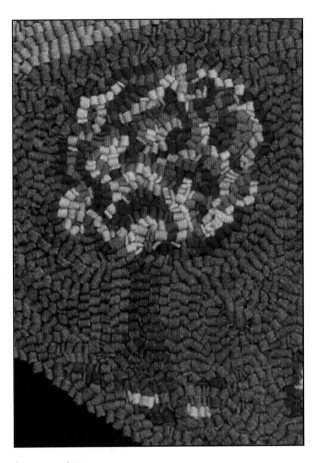

Close up of tree.

1.) Transfer the pattern onto your backing fabric. Refer to "Transferring Your Pattern." Finish the edges, referring to "Finishing the Edges to Prevent Unraveling" on page 16.

2. Begin hooking the church and hill as follows:

    line in the door and roofs – black
    trim – white
    windows – orange
    bell – gold
    bushes and trees – red, rust, yellow, and orange randomly
    building and steeple – yellow
    small path and tree trunks – brown
    grass – dark green

3.) Hook the blue house on the left hill as follows:

    trim – white
    windows – orange
    door – brown
    bushes – red, rust, yellow, and orange randomly
    house – blue
    roof – black
    chimney – rust
    hill – medium green

4.) Hook the 3 houses on the right hill as follows:

    windows and roofs – black
    doors – brown
    bushes – red, rust, yellow, and orange randomly
    left house – red
    middle house – blue
    back house – rust
    hill – light green

5.) Hook the clouds – white; hook the sky – mottled orange

6.) Outline "Faith" in gold, fill in with yellow. All the acorn tops are brown and the bodies are random greens. The outline and the vein on the leaves to the left are maroon, fill in with red. The outline and the vein on the leaves to the right are hooked in rust, fill in with orange. Outline "Family" with maroon, fill in with red. The outline and the vein on the leaves to the right are gold, fill in with yellow.

7.) The background is hooked in black.

8.) Block your rug following "Blocking Your Rug" on page 20.

9.) Finish the rug following "Whipstitching with cording" on page 20 or any of the other options in the "Finishing Your Rug" section on page 20.

10.) Block again following "Blocking Your Rug" on page 20.

French Horn Christmas Stocking

I have to thank Norma McElhenny and Diane Stoeffel for their input with this stocking. I brought it to an open workshop with one idea and left with a completely different idea that I absolutely loved. Classes are great places to pick up ideas and tips as well as socialize with other "hookers."

Finished size: 15 1/2" x 11"
#6 cut

Wool:

1/2 yard very dark green
12" x 24" gold
12" x 10" red
12" x 10" dark red
10" x 5" copper
10" x 5" dark green
10" x 5" light green
8" x 5" brown

Materials:

2/3 yard cotton material for lining

1.) Enlarge the pattern and transfer onto your backing fabric. Refer to "Transferring Your Pattern" on page 14. Finish the edges, referring to "Finishing the Edges to Prevent Unraveling" on page 16.

2.) Hook on the front petal lines with gold, fill in with red. Hook on the back petal lines with copper, fill in with dark red.

Hook the gold outline on the marked line.

58

The center is done by picking up two colors (green and copper) through one hole. Hold the two colors as one piece. Outline both the holly leaves and center veins with light green, fill in the holly leaves with dark green. To separate the poinsettia petals from the horn, hook a line of brown. This will also act as a shadow.

3.) Hook the mouthpiece and the stripe on the horn with copper. Hook the inside of the horn with brown. Hook the horn with gold.

4.) The berries are hooked in red – bring up a tail, bring up a loop, bring up another loop, and snip to leave a tail. The holly leaves are outlined with dark green and filled in with light green.

5.) Hook the background with very dark green.

6.) Block your finished design following the directions on page 20.

7.) Zigzag 1" from hooked design and cut away excess backing.

8.) Cut the stocking back from the remaining very dark green wool using the hooked stocking as a guide. Cut 2 lining pieces (one with the toe facing right, one with the toe facing left) using the hooked stocking as a guide.

Pull up two tails through one hole.

Pull up two loops through one hole.

With right sides together sew the lining piece to the stocking piece *along the top only*.
Repeat with the stocking back. Flatten out each piece.

9.) With the right sides together, sew the lining piece to the stocking *along the top only*. Repeat with the stocking back. Flatten out each piece.

10.) Cut a 1" x 5" tab out of green wool for hanging. With the right sides together, pin the hooked stocking to the wool stocking back and the linings together. Insert the folded tab between the hooked stocking layers at the upper right (to hang the stocking). The tab should be inserted far enough between the layers to be caught in the 1/2-inch seam allowance.

With right sides together, pin the hooked stocking to the wool stocking back and the linings together.

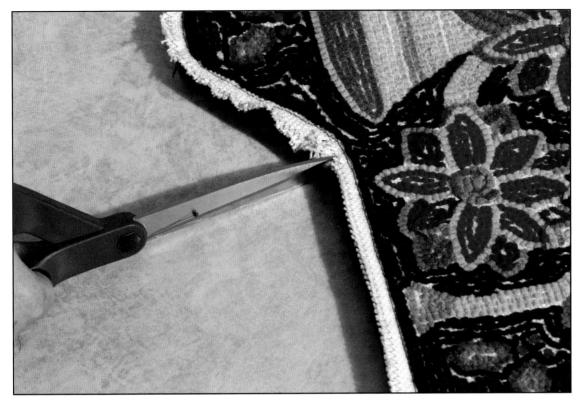

Snip the inside curve in the seam allowance.

11.) Sew with a 1/2" seam allowance, leaving a 6-8" opening at the bottom of the lining. Snip the inside curve (near the horn) in the seam allowance.

12.) Turn the stocking right side out through the opening. The hooked area will be a little stiff, but gentle coaxing will pull it through the opening. Whipstitch the open area closed. Push the lining into the stocking. Press flat and you're ready to fill with Christmas goodies!

Whip stitch the open area closed.

Sheep with Watermelon Wagon Rug

Finished size 37" x 27"
#5 cut

Wool:

1/2 yard black
1/2 yard white
3/8 yard total of brown
3/8 yard total of light gold/yellow
(2 different shades)
1/4 yard red
1/8 yard dark green
1/8 yard medium green
1/8 yard light green
10" x 4" very dark green
10" x 4" medium brown/gold
10" x 4" dark gold
10" x 4" medium gold
5" x 6" dark red
5" x 6" very dark brown

Materials:

45" x 35" backing fabric
4 oz. skein black wool yarn for binding
1 oz dark green wool yarn for binding

1.) Enlarge the pattern and transfer onto your backing fabric. Refer to "Transferring Your Pattern" on page 14. Finish the edges, referring to "Finishing the Edges to Prevent Unraveling."

2.) Hook the rug in the following order:

Barn trim – white (hook on lines)
Barn – red
Roofs – black
Star on sheep's blanket – light gold, medium gold
Sheep's blanket – red
Sheep's body – white
Sheep's eyes – brown
Sheep's legs, head, ears, tail – black
Watermelon wagon rind – 1 row of very dark green
Watermelon wagon inner rind – 2 rows of light green
Watermelon wagon white – 1 row of white
Seeds – black
Flesh – Red
Wheels – very dark brown (hook on lines)

All stems – brown

Grapes – light, medium, and dark greens

Apples – dark red, red, dark red

Pears – medium gold

Pineapple markings – brown

Pineapple – medium brown/gold

Pineapple top – very dark green and dark green

Outline whole watermelon – very dark green

Whole watermelon – medium green and white

Tree bark – brown

Leaves – dark green

3.) Hook the grass following the directions for "Meandering" on page 19 with light, medium, and dark green.

4.) Hook the sky following the directions for "Meandering" on page 19 with light gold/yellow.

5.) Dirt area is hooked from side to side with browns.

6.) Checkerboard pattern is hooked in black and white.

7.) Watermelon corners are hooked as follows:

Watermelon rind – 1 row of very dark green

Watermelon inner rind – 2 rows of light green

Watermelon white – 1 row of white (hook on line)

Seeds – black

Watermelon flesh – red

8.) Block your rug following "Blocking Your Rug" on page 20.

9.) Finish the rug following "whipstitching with cording" on page 20 or any of the other options in the Finishing Your Rug section. Whipstitch with black except for the corners. Switch to green for the corners.

10.) Block again following "Blocking Your Rug" on page 20.

Sheep Pillow

Finished size: 14" x 14"
#6 cut

Wool:

    1/6 yard white
    1/6 yard total dark and light green
    1/6 yard total light gold/yellow
    1/8 yard black
    10" x 14" red

Materials:

    21" x 21" backing fabric
    14 1/2" x 14 1/2" red fabric
    14" x 14" pillow form (or fiberfill for stuffing)

1.) Enlarge the pattern and transfer onto your backing fabric. Refer to "Transferring Your Pattern" on page 14. Finish the edges, referring to "Finishing the Edges to Prevent Unraveling" on page 16.

2.) Hook the sheep as follows:
    Sheep's body – white
    Sheep's eyes – brown
    Sheep's legs, head, ears, tail – black
Hook the sheep's blanket as follows:
    Watermelon rind – 1 row of dark green
    Watermelon inner rind – 1 row of light green
    Watermelon white – 1 row of white
    Seeds – black
    Watermelon flesh and bottom of blanket saddle – red

3.) Hook the grass following the directions for "Meandering" on page 19 with light, medium, and dark green.

4.) Hook the sky following the directions for "Meandering" on page 19 with light gold/yellow.

5.) Checkerboard pattern is hooked in black and white.

6.) Watermelon corners are hooked as follows:
    Watermelon rind – 1 row of dark green
    Watermelon inner rind – 1 row of light green
    Watermelon white – 1 row of white
    Seeds – black
    Watermelon flesh – red

7.) Block your rug following "Blocking Your Rug" on page 20.

8.) Zigzag 1" from hooked design and cut away excess.

9.) Place the right sides of the fabric and hooking together and stitch using a 1/2" seam allowance. Leave an 8" opening at the bottom to insert the pillow form. (Leave a smaller opening if you are using the fiberfill.) Trim excess fabric. Turn the pillow inside out. Push out the corners.

10.) Insert pillow form or fiberfill and whip-stitch the opening closed.

Watermelon Pillow

Finished size: 8 1/2" x 11"
#8 cut

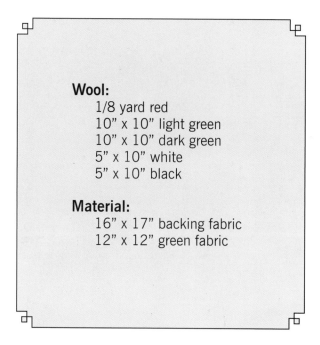

Wool:
1/8 yard red
10" x 10" light green
10" x 10" dark green
5" x 10" white
5" x 10" black

Material:
16" x 17" backing fabric
12" x 12" green fabric

1.) Enlarge the pattern and transfer onto your backing fabric. Refer to "Transferring Your Pattern" on page 14. Finish the edges, referring to "Finishing the Edges to Prevent Unraveling" on page 16.

2.) Hook the seeds with black, the flesh in red. Hook on the rind line with white, two rows of light green, two rows of dark green.

3.) Block your rug following "Blocking Your Rug" on page 20.

4.) Zigzag 1" from hooked design and cut away excess backing.

5.) Cut out the back fabric using the hooked design as a pattern.

6.) Place the right sides of the fabric and hooking together and stitch using a 1/2" seam allowance. Leave a 3" opening at the bottom to insert the fiberfill. Trim excess fabric. Turn the pillow inside out. Push out the corners.

7.) Insert fiberfill and whipstitch the opening closed.

Eye Mask

Finished size: 9" x 5"
#6 cut

Wool:

    1/6 yard peach wool
    12" x 4" blue (or your eye color) wool
    12" x 4" black wool
    12" x 4" white wool
    6" x 4" dark peach wool

Materials:

    17" x 13" backing fabric
    15" x 11" flannel
    white carpet thread
    peach sewing thread
    1/2" x 15" elastic

1.) Transfer the pattern onto your backing. Refer to "Transferring Your Pattern" on page 20. Finish the edges, referring to "Finishing the Edges to Prevent Unraveling" on page 20.

2.) Hook as follows:

    pupils – black
    iris – blue (or your eye color)
    white of the eye – white
    eyelashes – black
    around eyes and nose – dark peach
    face – peach

3.) Zigzag 1" from hooked design and cut away excess backing.

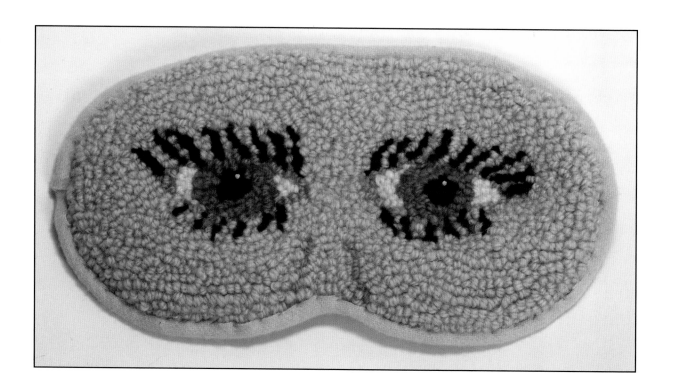

4.) With the carpet thread and a large eye sewing needle, make a good size knot. On the hooked side, run the needle slightly right of center and let the knot "sit" on the hooking to make a highlight. Secure by knotting on the back. Repeat for the other eye – again slightly right of center. You can also do this as a French knot.

5.) Cut out the eye mask backing fabric using the hooked design as a pattern.

6.) Place wrong sides together and zigzag as close to the hooked area as possible with a tight zigzag. Cut away excess area to 1/4" of the hooking.

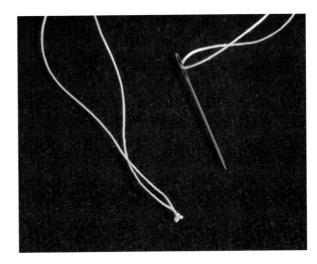

Knot the carpet thread.

Place the knot slightly left of center on the pupil.

7.) Cut a strip of wool 30" x 2". Piece following the instructions on page 23 if necessary. Make a bias tape by folding one side in 1/4". Fold the other side in 1/4". Fold both sides together.

Fold in one side 1/4".

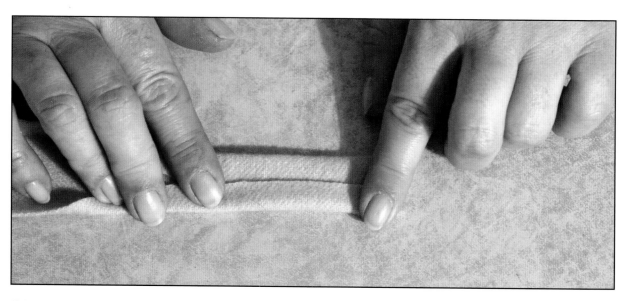

Fold in the other side 1/4".

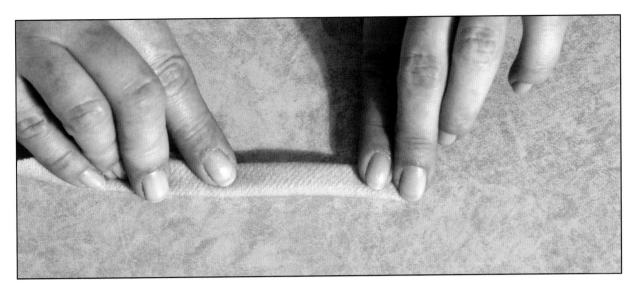

Fold both sides together.

8.) Sandwich the eye mask between the bias tape starting in a side area. Pin bias tape in place.

Place one edge of the bias under the zigzag.

Sandwich the eye mask between the bias tape.

9.) From the backside, bring your needle with the peach thread up as close to the hooking as possible. Catch the edge of the bias tape. Bring the needle down as close to the hooking as possible. Catch the edge of the bias tape on the back. Repeat all the way around the mask.

From the backside, bring your needle with the peach thread up as close to the hooking as possible.

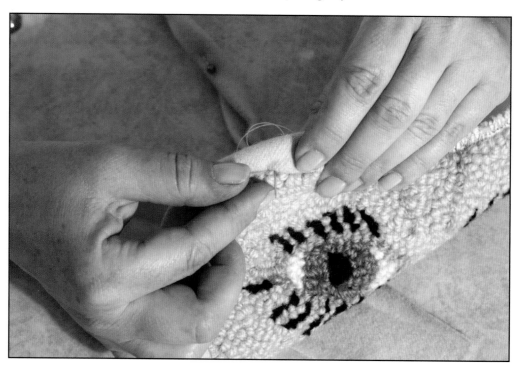

Catch the edge of the bias tape.

74

Bring the needle down to the back as close to the hooking as possible.

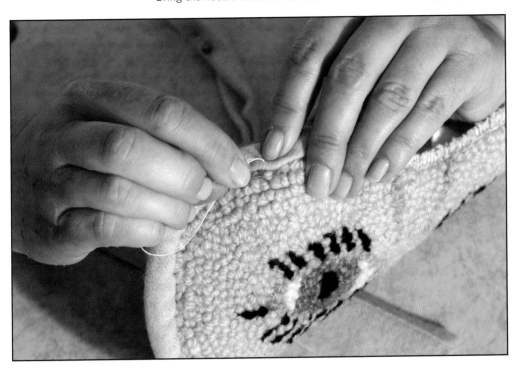

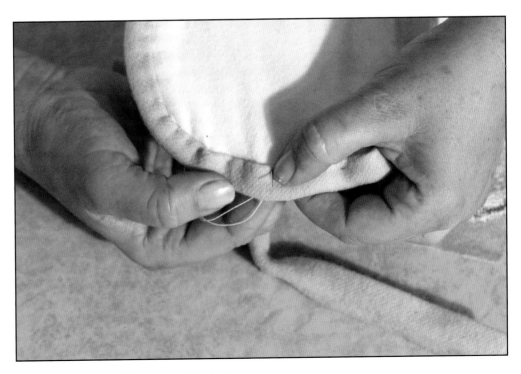

Catch the edge of the bias tape on the back.

10.) Attach the elastic to each side.

Attach elastic to the sides.

Spohr Garden

A hidden gem on Cape Cod, Spohr Gardens is a 6 acre garden located on Oyster Pond in Falmouth, Massachusetts. Mr. and Mrs. Charles Spohr purchased the land in 1950. Throughout the years they have put in paths and thousands of plants and trees and opened the area to the public. Anchors, bells, millstones, and architectural items are beautifully displayed around the foliage. This is a fabulous spot for a wedding or just a stroll.

Spohr Gardens is located at 45 Fells Road, Falmouth, MA 02540, phone 508-540-0623, or www.spohrgardens.org.

Patterns

Americana Stair Treads
Enlarge 370%

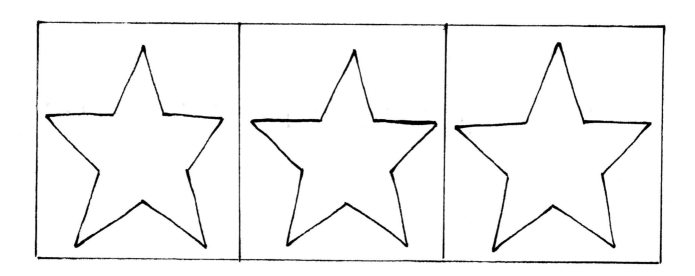

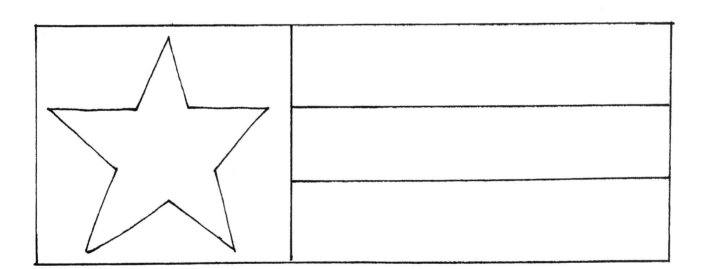

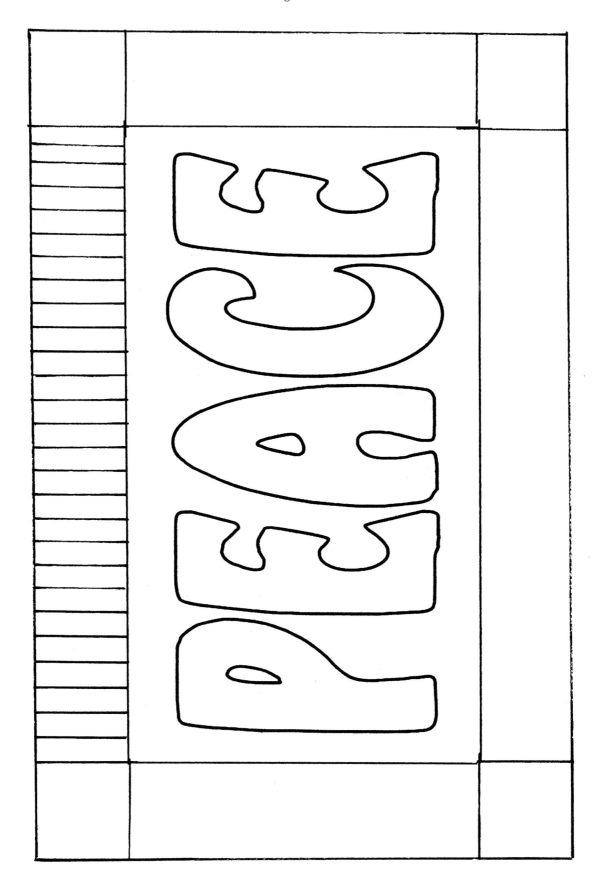

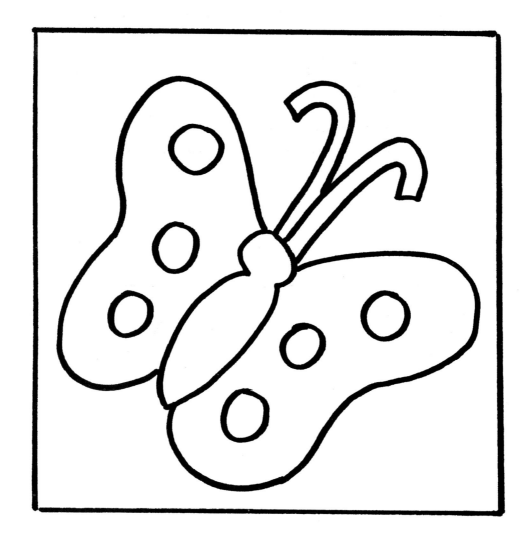

Play Pillow
Enlarge 300%

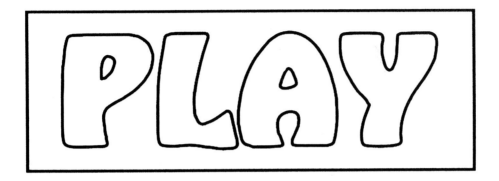

Dream Pillow
Enlarge 300%

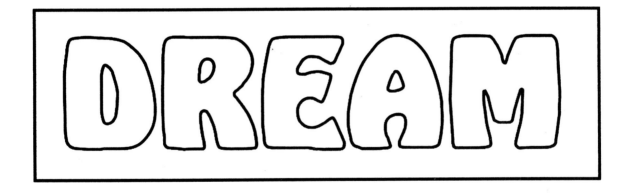

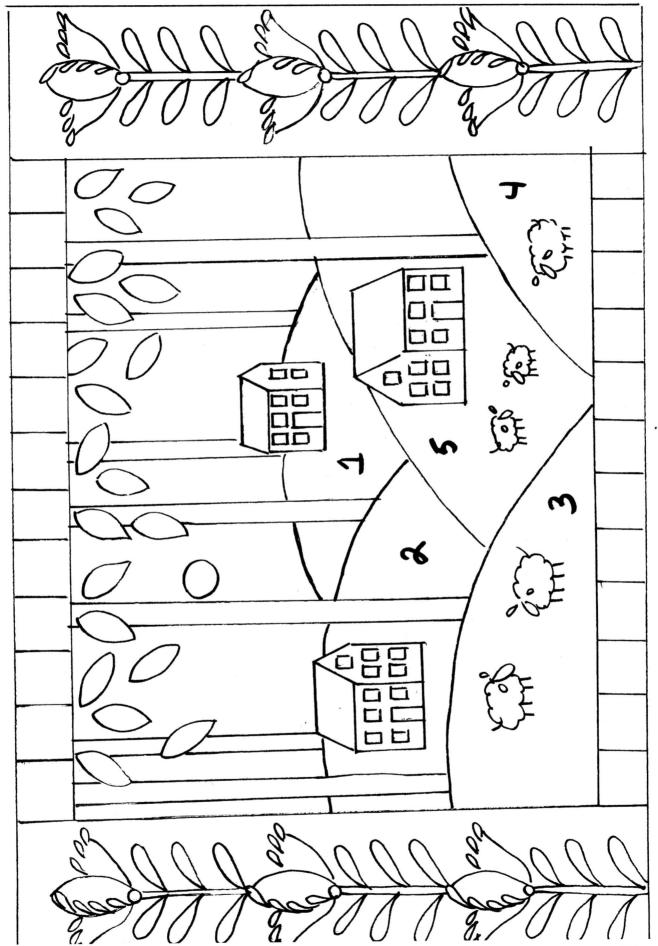

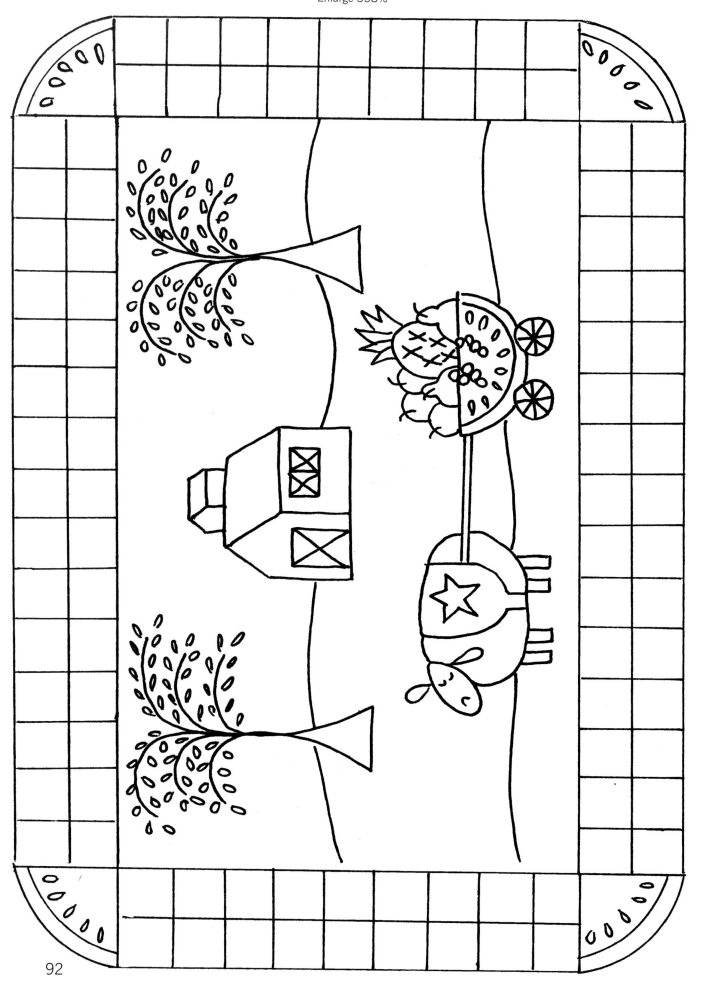

Sheep Pillow
Enlarge 127%

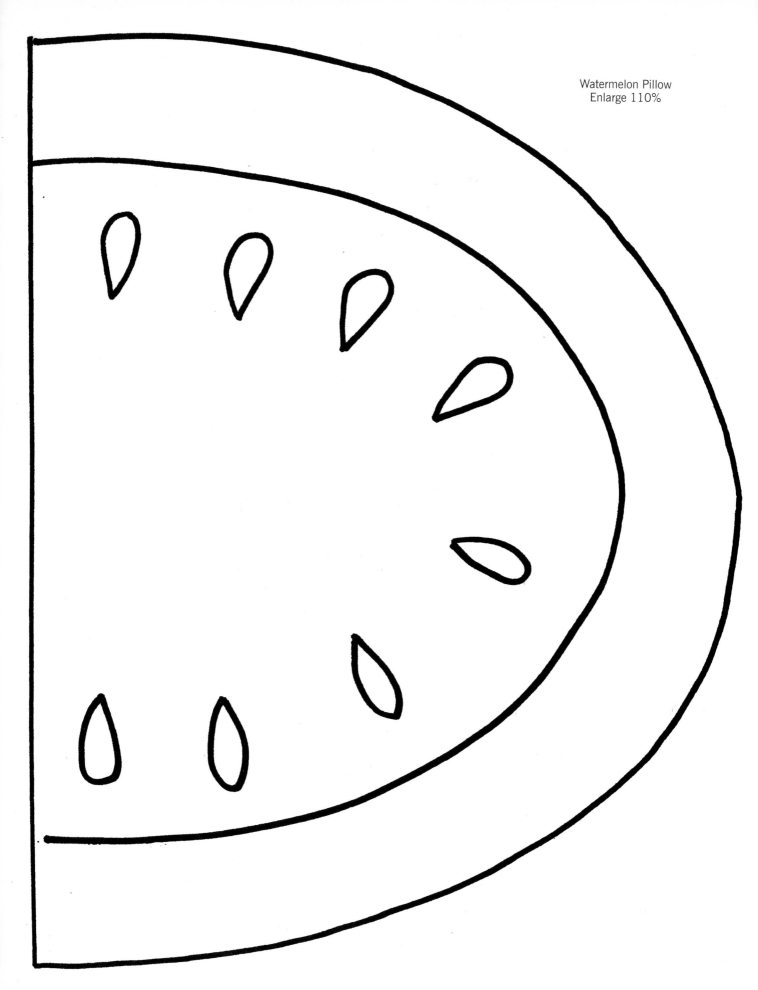

Watermelon Pillow
Enlarge 110%

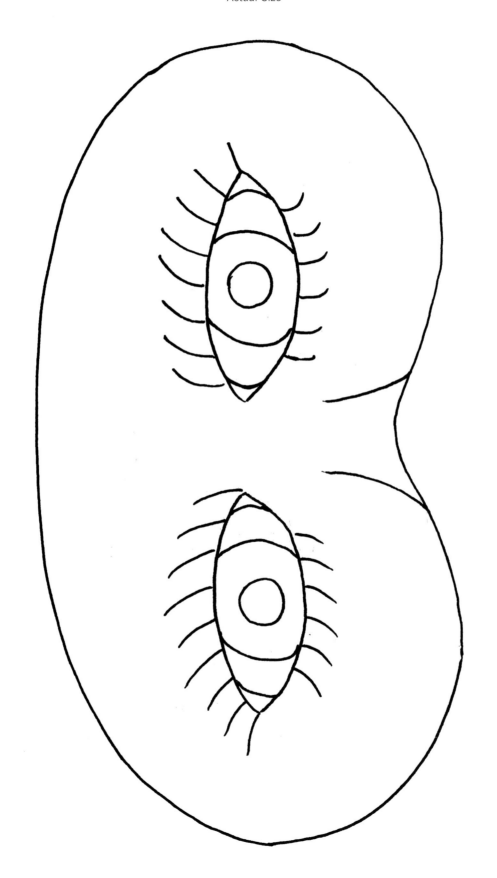

References and Resources

Magazines and Books

ATHA (Association of Traditional Hooking Artists)
Joan Cahill, Membership Chairman
600 Maple Street
Endicott, NY 13760
607-748-7588
www.atharugs.com

Rug Hooking Magazine
1300 Market Street, Suite 202
Leymoyne, PA 17043-1420
800-233-9055
www.rughookingonline.com

The Wool Street Journal
312 North Custer
Colorado Springs, CO 80903
888-784-5667
www.woolstreetjournal.com

Cross, Pat. *Purely Primitive: Hooked Rugs from Wool, Yarn, and Homespun Scraps.* Woodinville, Washington: Martingale & Company, 2003.
Mather, Anne D. *The Art of Rug Hooking.* New York: Sterling Publishing Company, Inc., 1999.
Siano, Margaret with Susan Huxley. *Secrets of Finishing Hooked Rugs.* Lemoyne, Pennsylvania: Rug Hooking Magazine, 2003.

Supplies

Full size patterns preprinted on monk's cloth, wools, and yarns shown in this book along with new patterns for rug hooking, wool appliqué, punch needle, and painting can be purchased by visiting my website at www.christinebrault.com or contact me at Jansenbrault@aol.com.

Ault's Rug Hooking Store
4515 Laser Road
Shelby, Ohio 44875
419-347-9957
866-659-1752
www.aults.com
Cutters, hooks, wool, and more.

Dorr Mill Store
PO Box 88
Guild, NH 03754
800-846-3677
www.dorrmillstore.com
Dyeing supplies, hooks, wool.

Halcyon Yarn
12 School Street
Bath, ME 04530
800-341-0282
www.halcyonyarn.com
Rug yarn, hooks, backing fabrics, dyeing supplies.

Harry M. Fraser Company
433 Duggins Road
Stoneville, NC 27049
336-673-9830
www.fraserrugs.com
Cutters, hooks, backing fabrics.

Pro Chemical & Dye
PO Box 14
Somerset, MA 02726
800-2-BUY-DYE
www.prochemical.com
Dyeing supplies.

W. Cushing & Company
P.O. Box 351
21 North Street
Kennebunkport, ME 04046
www.wcushing.com
Dyeing supplies, hooks, backing fabrics, and more.

Disclaimer

The information in this book is presented in good faith, but no warranty is given nor results guaranteed. The written instructions, designs, projects, photographs, and patterns are intended for personal, noncommercial use of the retail consumer and are under federal copyright laws. No part of this book may be reproduced in any form. Permission is granted to photocopy patterns for personal use of the retail consumer.